Science And

•—•—•

Diane Furtney

FUTURECYCLE PRESS

www.futurecycle.org

Cover photo, "Barnard's Galaxy, also known as NGC 6822," courtesy of ESO/José Francisco (josefrancisco.org); cover and interior book design by Diane Kistner (dkistner@futurecycle.org); Gentium Book Basic text with Chalkboard titling

Published by FutureCycle Press
Hayesville, North Carolina, USA

ISBN 978-1-938853-30-2

In memory of Gayle Furtney
(1954-2004)

Contents

I

Science And Family

Lithium, Chromium

Sand and sugars in deep space; interstellar
water arranging itself into something cellular

by means of a cold membrane
around each molecule; black lanes

of clouds inside star groups replete
with silicon and the beauty grit

of carbon; ions horsing around on comets;
every light in the sky beyond this planet

arriving from a sibling
or subtle cousin or prosperous, helloing

Auntie Mame from the Big Bang;
colored baubles over a crib; old and young

magnetars braiding spacetime in plaits
to the edge of the cosmos; re- and re-restated

explosions, friction, ratios
of pressure and temperature, E-I-E-I-O,

clay-crystal rings, mineral alliances
in the air and underfoot; apparent distances,

apparent isolation, but no object
actually in disconnect—

re-bondings, titanic things moving in thrall
to the strong force at the level

of the nuclear; a silent din
overhead from templates of hemoglobin

and new skin: physics and chemistry
are difficult, they are entirely about family.

A Man, A Boy, A Stick, A Goose With Goslings

To J., who asked during a dinner outing (after an afternoon drive and birding in Ohio), "What about you? Do you want that rescue?"

A crowd, at blue-checked tablecloths.
A wall of old white windows, one corner lath

showing through. Our table, one of five, juts
toward deal chairs that abut

a plywood bar earnest about its dozen brands,
tended by eager local boys who try to stand

like sophisticates but look like extremely nice
children. Sugar dispenser, flip-top lid. A brace

of red and yellow squeeze bottles.
Four chairs for us, cushioned, mottled,

on two of which our purses perch
like nesting birds. This was once a church,

the menu says; earlier a mill. Now a rural eatery
prized for weekend fish and chicken dinners, a leafy

five miles east of Sidney—old Erie Canal
quarry town in the Western Reserve, with pastel

courthouse and extravagant Sullivan bank.
Clatter; laughs. A high-school hostess, frank-

faced, blonde, who's sorry about the wait.
Families are in line from the back gravel lot

toward the front veranda, out of sight.
And beyond our wide window, the late

May grass, carrying scattered trees,
slopes down to the Great Miami's

pebbles and water, a hundred feet wide.
Well-behaved trees on the other side

layer themselves up a hill, to rounded clouds.
At left, from a sandbar that fingers down

the river, a great blue heron advances
over the shallows, its neck like a branch

whittled to a spear. Now, a dart
of white wing, below our

soundless window glass:
a commotion and flutter on the grass.

Five goslings, water-tumbler-sized,
yellow, wobbly, solemn, fuzzed,

streaked in May with the colors of autumn,
on rubbery charcoal feet, are in a scrum

behind their hooting, nervous father goose,
who doesn't like the surly boy who's

trapped a separated gosling, is about
to pick it up. The parent bird, stretching out

his neck at the predator, the Breaker of Babies,
has flapped his white wings, head down. No doubt he's

hissing like a huge, good teapot.
And the human father shoulders in from the parking lot,

far left. Dark-haired. Late thirties.
Nondescript clothes. Not bad looking. He's

yelled something, scowling at his son;
picked up a six-foot stick; is advancing on

the terrified goose with a shoulder-rolling eagerness
that says everything about his loose,

unloved history. The bird faces this Monster
with wings outstretched. His babies scatter

behind him: he has told them to run.
And for women looking out these windows, even

those who sympathize with or fear
for the man, several things are clear:

that the boy, as you observe, "needs rescue
only from his Dad"; that the Thrasher of Stick came too

tardily for dinner, had to wait in line, resents his son,
and now has a chance to hurt something, someone.

It's clear, too, he's unhappily married,
is unexceptional if not bad in bed,

and it's his own brutalizing father he's turned into,
a man he hated—bibbety-bobbity-boo.

No woman, though, can tap this glass
with authority, to stop him. No man here wants the mess

of intervention, an end-of-the-week
argument. Ah! but now the stick

is gone: he's tossed it with a wide flail,
a pretense at contempt. (He is not, after all,

entirely sure who owns those birds.
Besides, the goose is big.) He turns toward

the lot and his hand has momentum-swing
as he pushes his offspring,

who now no doubt has learned
something already learned, learned, learned.

What if some of it could be unlearned?
If we could unscar the burned-

in tissue-patterns from our early lives,
those auto-jerk neurons that do us no good? I've

come across, say, a longer-lasting amine
to boost some synapses in the brain—

down in the quick-memory hippocampus
and old amygdala—to revamp us

by allowing for emotional renewal.
Maybe a hormone, Change-a-trol,

for plasticity in the cortex, setting us free,
a little, from our iron-track loyalty

to the inept parenting we endured... This salt shaker
—glass, aluminum-capped—on this blue square:

suppose it offers an option for the human race.
Pick it up and you'll have made a choice

for neuronal newness to be offered to that Son
of Stick (and to everyone) at, say, twenty-one,

by which age that particular boy
may already have married for the first time, O boy,

and be vigorously reproducing his Dad.
"Who will re-teach him?" For now, let's set aside

that good question (recalling that for millions of us,
socialization might have been better done by mollusks).

As he de- and re-learns, could a chemical light
evaporate the damp edges of a bright,

less-hampered self, the categories
of suffering become the categories

of rescue, and hope leap outward to a huge perimeter?
There's no need, of course—is there?—

to wonder what other forms of animate matter
might prefer, what would be their

knowledgeable choice for us. Every phylum on this planet
would scramble and burst out of its habitat

in a rush for that salt shaker,
the biggest stampede in the history of cell structure.

That dream you once had, remember—of being renewed?
And me, you ask? Do I "want that rescue?"

See me pushing the brass plate on the clinic door.
See my pen pressing the forms ("Your

treatment goal?" *"To be a bit more anserine*
and much less like a man once seen

outside a window.") And you, who's said that error
is "the hand-me-down from every mother":

if those mistakes could lose their intense
pressure—with your well-raised daughter, for instance:

to see on her face a look of fresh assessment,
see a smile that's rueful or indifferent

in its forgiveness, and know that some deep decibels
of your old call to her are barely audible

and that she's not smaller for her loss, your loved girl—
would you then have a less warm world,

or more? There's a slight chill now across the floor:
today's Full-grown Misery has come in the front door.

He's yanking, on an invisible leash,
his hangdog son, then his abashed

and run-down wife, for whom none of this is new.
Given a second chance, what might *she* do?

Meanwhile, the heron has flipped
and gulleted his dinner. Re-dignified, he's stepped,

as you say, "like a new graduate,"
up the sandbar toward the woods. The baked

perch looks excellent. Our good waitress, bonhomous
and bouncy, is penciling nearby. The gorgeous

water that striped past moments ago
has already dropped toward the Ohio

and by Monday will have reached the Gulf.
Are those enough?

Endurance, a pleasant this and that, the pretty glare
of occasional achievement—enough? Or,

to arrive at and keep the decency of a goose.
Here's the salt shaker (a little sticky)... What would you choose?

The Carboniferous

There were mazes of roots. Bright red
beach sand. Eggy mud.

The moon was closer to the Earth
and circling faster, always north

of the one, flat continent
of almost-zero gradient

across twenty-five hundred miles at the equator.
A month was twenty days. The pole star

was in Draco then, among L-shaped
stars that had been dipper-shaped

five times and would close
into dipper shape again. Bellows

and grunts out of the water, in daytime.
Along the surf-edge, parallel lines

of log-sized proto-salamanders and thirty-pound
paleo-frogs, twelve feet long. The round,

transparent sacs hanging from shore roots
were new-laid placodonts with minute,

six-toed legs and tiny spots of fangs.
Damselflies had three-foot wings,

mayflies weighed two pounds; bristletails
and sowbugs, a foot long, wore metallic scales

and waxy cuticle so as not to drown in the air.
Day and night: clackings and stutter,

zuzz and whines, or the *pok pok*
of spiders' carapaces when they knocked

on shelled insects stumbling into their webs.
Across the big roots, trip-wire webs

were single strands; more webs, quarter-inch sheets,
were strung to sixty feet

between the wall-to-wall trees.
Those trees: short and spongy

or hollow and reedy and tall,
wrapped with leaves half the size of a fingernail

or bare-stemmed with tassels
out the top. —What else?

There was green and green
and gray and green,

and three things that were white:
the face-on moon, the tall, bright

clouds floating on a continent
of oxygen—a third of the air then—

oxygen so deep it hazed and grayed the sea;
and white from the crinoid lilies

a few feet underwater, in meadows, waving
on stalks, their acres paving

the seabeds out toward every horizon.
The seas were four feet to fifteen,

but deep on the other side of the globe;
little difference between ebb

and tide, and the water had less salt. Things
sank fast. The trees kept moving

from the beaches into the ocean-bogs,
by the millions, turning into peat-sog

in a few weeks, into coal in a few years,
miles deep. Inland? Up and down the mire

and hummocks were arching cycads,
three-foot scorpions, seed-fern mazes with bicuspid-

sized pollen on ten-foot straps
—and a weird acoustic, from traps

of carbon dioxide sinking through the tight
canopy; a clayish light.

Other things? —arrive only in dreams
or odd moments: the boom

of wind three times a day, straight
and horizontal, just ahead of the straight-

down rain. Depending on the sun's
position, looping sections

of the longest webs would rainbow, later,
in the mist. But the pads that cluttered

the still lagoons: were they yellow
or brown? There are slow

extinctions of outlook. Everyone remembers
how the divisions of time—"September,"

"March"—were imposed from elsewhere,
like other categories. There were years

of reorderings and reassessments
that pressed the bottom layers. Then, plants

with odor and covered seeds; birds,
mammals—another world,

moving across and over the old, drumming climate,
which had been islanded by that

growing pressure throughout the Interlude,
the decade-long era of mid-childhood.

The Real

For Gong-Chi, biochemist, who dismissed the idea that
serious information might arrive from dreams, adding
cheerfully, "I wish to know what is real."

When I lived in San Francisco—a twelve-year
period across my thirties—there was a peculiar

set of days: about a week. I'd planned,
as an exercise, to draft a short description,

the urgency of which down-pressed
on me suddenly, became a demand or test.

I was to detail the almost-daily way,
from age four until eighteen, I ran away

from the shrill, peering, punitive, depressed,
frantically conventional, self-obsessed

woman, my mother, whose house—near Trenton
Avenue in Tulsa—I was required to stay in,

for some reason, and return to after school.
(Who, I wondered at six, made up that rule?

There were lots of houses, in lines
under lots of old trees; why

not go to one of them?) To get away—for
minutes, an hour, longer, late for dinner,

half a day gone—to the tangled regions
of nearby, wild Joe Creek, its forts and paths—would mean,

in barefoot summer, having to make
four painful, running jumps across the baked

and bubble-blistered tarmac of Trenton.
—I began the draft, but in days of block and then

uneasiness that rose and rippled like heat,
things began to happen. I spilled tea

—a large mug, boiling—across my foot,
this on my cocktail job, where I also cut

my hand. Next day I left my coin purse
at a grocery store, went back and first

noticed the hairstyle of the checkout clerk
was like my own in high school. I worked

my shifts, but barely. Sleeping badly,
I then scarred my right wrist, badly,

with an iron—this on day three,
when my breath became shallow, periphery

objects such as buses and cars
weren't always noticed, and I didn't hear

or remember much what people said.
Back in my rooms that night, I grew afraid

that in the morning I wouldn't cross the fence
of streets—not safely—that joined my apartment

to my simple job. In the interior,
something Terrible was near.

I had nothing to lose, then, I thought,
if I spoke to the surroundings, to that

live Darkness. Between the subdued sheets
—it was dark at the windows, late—

I imagined stepping to
the farthest back room of the mind, to

its empty wall and heavy door, where
I was lifting up an iron bar

and calling down the stairs
—unlit, steep—to anything: powers,

allies, sub-selves, auxiliaries:
"Please come up. Help me.

I'm weak, I might not live. I'm lost.
Please come—in any shape, at any cost.

I'll listen, I will pay attention."
I may have said this aloud, I may have been

in tears. And on the table
of dreams, I waited for the Terrible.

What came was amphibian, a toad, almost
at eye level. Partway under a house,

it crouched on a line that traced
where light met the shadow of the crawlspace.

Big, it stared at me, motionless,
without experience of powerlessness,

without entreaty: ambassadorial,
empowered in two worlds, while

"It's like a rock with eyes,"
the dream said. —In the morning noise

and glare of the workaday world in sea air,
when, unsteady and nervous, it occurred

to me to say aloud, "Like a rock with eyes"
and I did so, there was a surprise:

at once I was more calm. At
21st and Anza, I said the phrase again and got

across the street. Amid antique tables and stools
and the chic, terrified ethic of cool,

I printed "Like a rock with eyes" on a bar
napkin, propped it on the register,

whispered it now and then, and met with no
injury. The tarmac described itself in a day or so,

what had been one project broke, clean-edged,
into two, then gradually enlarged,

without heat or threat. —Gong-Chi,
you're a kind woman, now embarrassed for me;

you think I have disclosed too much.
I think what I've disclosed is such

an everyday process the human brain
seldom bothers to describe it to itself. —The green

microwave near my office now heats our tea.
Around it, and your wet bench, and the galaxy,

other matter invisibly
extends, also usefully

and real: heavy, mobile,
engaged in certain shapings and control,

emitting no light, responsive
only to the largest force, and if

pushed, pushes back, squat
and incompressible, both of this world and not.

Horizons

"Sometimes justice is too much to hope for"
—from a history of the Crimean War

A boy of sixteen finds his father
self-hanged from a pipe in his brick coal cellar

under ongoing ranting from a harridan
family matriarch—this during the Depression,

in St. Louis. Before that afternoon,
the limit of possibilities, the emotional horizon

around the boy, might have been distant,
large. But—to some extent

by choice?—he then went deep into an interior,
took up the enterprises of a Midwest engineer,

and cultivated stasis and violence.
By thirty, his relationships were tense,

binding obligations to himself, permitting
evasions, tyranny-rages, his unremitting

intimidation, spousal rape ("You have to! You signed
the marriage contract!"). But, because time

moves in a straight line through us, the justice
of biology, of development, is

that every action, with or without thought,
reorganizes and delimits what can be brought

into the future, including one's ability to know it.
By his forties, the horizon edge of his possibilities fit

around his region, then his township;
not even bouts of sudden illness could strip

or prise his habits. He learned no new subject,
was bored by nature, sniggered at the projects

of art, was irritated and baffled by
the concept of empathy,

and permitted no approach. Those most
in need of him outwaited their need, in the slowest

of developments: from fear and solitary panic
to negotiations (thwarted), then monotonic

confusion and flounderings; later, the automatic
courtesy reserved for strangers, mixed with analytic

pity; nearer the end, a numbed indifference.
By his sixties, none of his children would consent

to emplace him in the future; none
of the four would have a child. His horizon

finally, at eighty-seven, gripped
his identity like a mummy's wrap,

his self-absorption so complete, so assiduous,
there was no need—tending his needs—for anyone else

to give him an invested thought. "Justice"
does not have to be hoped for; it is ubiquitous

and emergent. It will not rhyme with "mercy,"
"love," "wish," or other forms of clemency;

it rhymes, every moment, with "frame,"
"balance," "decision," "sadness," and with the name

of every peace or war, including the Crimean.
The name of his cemetery? No one has any idea.

Spherical Eversion

To myself, wondering whether it wouldn't be better to avoid
more sibling encounters—just stop this sorry history, these
cross-purposes, this acrimony

It looked like acrimony,
like impatience and gratuitous, bony

betrayals. It sounded like calls
cut short, shouting in corridors, partial

apologies followed by sarcasm,
niched little silences for years, *in terrorem*

clauses, and the thrust of
more non-followings-through. So it was love

in process, stubborn love
using the engines of de-love

along the routes toward whatever re-love
there might be sudden room for. Shoves

from side to side: we were
girl-boy-girl-boy siblings, four,

trying quotidianly all our lives
to divide, with a blunted knife,

the single pea of parental
affect. It would all look, then, like maul

and mess, decade after decade of unclearness.
But it was always love, it was dearness,

dearness.
For each of us,

to reach a unique-enough location
would be like performing the eversion

of a sphere, for which a hypothesis
and imagination are required. Four successes

of a sort did result—professionalisms
and non-insane citizenships, with our schisms

acknowledged and loudly called across
before the end of living. Too, there was

the occasional moment of mutual clarity
about the rules of living, which apply themselves with charity

rarely, rules austere as axioms, including
that we were curved parallel lines, each in

love's motion, which has to exclude reverse,
and that meet on the far side of the universe.

— II —
Science And Romance

This One

How did it happen, this
unlikeliness?

An emphasis
in your past, was it, or mine, so a crisis

was step-asideable? What criss-
crossed, considering the rigor mortis

of my adolescence and the non-bliss
of yours, followed by labored learning's slow osmosis

for two decades after that? The x-axis
dots somehow met the axis

of y, with the current bright result. And I know this
much: it's all "huh?" and "whatsis?"

to me. You say you dunno, either. Genesis,
meanwhile, is

all that anyone longs to know about: the first basis
of the body, of those parents over there, of this

sphere in space, or anything that is
changing, such as, oh, the Coriolis

effect on the breeze, or a shift in stasis
so feeling can begin, including this

one, emphatic as clematis
rickracking now across the backyard trellis.

A quick crushing: is
that what the facts are doing—resynthesis

in a micromoment as the past compresses
into the one fat dot of "This Is

It"? So a back-of-the-neck kiss
and a bronze recovered below the Acropolis

connect instantly to the Lewis
and Clark expedition, the total Kiwanis

membership, and a recipe with orris?
Eventually, because my secret name was Limnanthis

(in my twenties) and since you like waffles, is
it certain we'd happen, without work or promises?

Bright Thing Across A Bright Table

To J.

Lately you've felt the weight, I think,
of superfluousness; at the brink

of late middle age felt the drub
of extraneousness like a club

in the night against your heart.
A fine daughter and grandson cart

away, this very minute,
part of your body into the future, and yet

the body of your hopes stays a little
bruised. The percentile ranking, meanwhile,

of your Life Accomplishment Quotient
gleams so golden and so argent,

there are probably few your uneasy
state could be confided to and seriously

believed. Look at you. Thing of unstable
and stable matter. Bright thing across a bright table.

Only the first two vacuums,
false and true, those fat, tiny rooms

that were the early Universe,
amounted to Necessity: unsuperfluous,

unique, relentlessly meaningful.
Since then nothing has been really full

or thoroughly significant.
Much more about which, though, I can't

tell you, being material
myself. However, if they were tracked, your serial

trajectories—the steady blaze
of infrared, say, or electron rays

emanating off the assorted quarks of you
as if from a sparking, still-new

dynamo—well, I'd have to accessorize
with special spectacles while your blue eyes

fraternize with nova swirls
and star-jets and emission shells,

luminosities micro- and stupendous,
each non-vacuumlike and therefore, yes, gratuitous,

in no way unlike yourself: of necessity
just beaming and gorgeous. Love me?

Blue Starred

To J., who will ask what took me so long in the yard

A few blocks away, downtown,
a train crossing the river holds down,

again and again, a complex chord on
some huge accordion.

The notes waver off toward
mostly empty air. There are no clouds.

Consolidated, blue stillness moves
straight to the moon. Above

the maple branches it's so clear
the upper atmosphere has disappeared.

Which might be a fluke of the climbing
half moon, or of this winding

breeze, cool and slotting like a key,
it feels like, through the lattice of this body,

then blowing into the spaces
of other meshworks nearby: the interstices

that add up to a slatted fence,
a trumpet creeper vine, a cat that in silence

is stepping onto the gravel drive, and insect
instars asleep in the nets

of the ground. Five billion years
before this night, a blue star, rare,

supermassive, nearby and boiling,
probably on this spiral arm but possibly roiling

out from the nearest curve of the Perseus,
blew up. In this direction, the concuss

of its shock wave
surrounded and concaved

a standing cloud of primordial hydrogen.
As the cloud condensed

to an oblong, it was stirred throughout
with blue-star bits. The grout

of angular drag and slow glue of gravity
flattened the cloud to a disk that eddied

into rounding points: comets
and bolides and running planets

around an igniting sun,
each of their separate evolutions

always another version of the carbon-
oxygen-nitrogen proportions

only a giant blue
in nova condition can produce

—reassembled of late into the soft and hard
arrangements in this cube of a yard,

its blood and wood. And one glowing day,
my love, when the sun is blowing away

and a similar if warmer breeze
has begun to rotate its long, slender keys,

we and other blue-star particles
will loosen in our Tinkertoy mesh and travel

into wider space again
—stay close to me, I'll stay close if I can—

arcing out in ionized light,
freebooting amidst bits of this white

moon, en route to our heirs, the next
and heavier-metal mix

of planets and star and eventual awarenesses
in their temporary solitudes: the endlessness

of being caught in shapes
and being freed. Including now the shape

of a sound carried back on the breeze
from under the Norway maple tree's

squared leaves, where last night's cricket (or
is it another?) calls again (more

urgently?) out from some ease or some crisis
in the blue and white grass.

● — III — ●

Science And The Homo Sapiens Young

And Snails

To a family friend (teenaged, female) viewing sodium and
potassium ions streaming out and into the pores of a cell
at a million transactions per second

Froglike things lolling on the seashore—twelve
feet long, chubby, fanged, and long-lived

in the Devonian—mixed with shelves
of mountain powder that in the past were not alive,

mostly, but parts of which, as calcium, had been alive
and slowly gliding during the last twelve

days of the most recent Appalachian uplift, then alive
again for a day or two after being blended, as twelve

quadrillion sugar ions, into a springtail swarm in the twelfth
century; all of the above

stirred with spice nubs, dogfish, orange groves,
and the pod of seal pups that shoved

and barked and flapped in 1912
on the Bering ice: everything that ever lived,

plus everything that never lived
or has not lived

yet but will: that's what girls and boys are made of.
It could almost be a template for—what? A sort of love?

The Good

*To a family friend (teenaged, male), annoyed by the length
of a murder trial entering its third week of deliberations*

Say you're the foreman of a jury. The issue
is the deaths of almost-finished tissue

growing in a vat: a factory bucket of nine
humans, gene-engineered to have no pain

at subzero temperatures and no cell freeze,
part of a project to colonize

the slopes of ice-volcano Herder
on Enceladus. The defendant, charged with murder,

deliberately opened the vat drains. Still-burdened
woman, she wept at what she saw then,

for what was and wasn't and might have been.
Your charge, though, is not to assess her emotions,

which, like all of ours, resemble heavy water
and will change in the future,

as will those of the maintenance crew
who came in on Monday and had to do

the floors, or what the factory owner
now feels, ruined as a contractor,

a man known for his optimism and resplendent
philanthropy. What measurement

can you use, not for what she hated
or hoped or feared, but for what she did?

Our best measures come from the body:
the one-yard stride, the ten-degree

fist, the foot—and now, at 5.7 feet,
the double-helix molecule. What's right,

what's wrong, action and relation, will all
refer eventually, and defer, to that molecule

as the one thing that might change
our past (with its strange

ancestral forms that flared
without direction or plan) after the snare

of current knowledge loosens,
widens, as it might when news

from accumulated variants
of DNA arrives. Invariant

now are decrepitude, early death, and threats
to everything inside the pretty habitat

of our tumultuous Local Bubble.
Whatever prods, then, the double molecule

and moves it—at any risk that's less
than certainty—into far-off niches

where it can redesign for decades,
centuries, sub- and newly speciated,

is what will become the universal good.
As prosecutor, I'd claim any deed

that levels our spiral staircase or props it
to go nowhere on one world, is the opposite

of good, is a form of murder
of our past as well as our future,

while an act that adds to the molecular good
allows two things: species adulthood

and a destiny worth the name.
Meanwhile, suppose the defendant's name

is Gwen. As you hear her defense,
know that you too constrict and fence

the future by what you do
to her and therefore to the two

next-generation bearers of the molecule
whom she has raised and is still

influencing (on this, week seven
of sequestered deliberations),

whom she cherishes and may well fear
for the future of, looking at the jury of her peers.

IV

Science And Irritation

The Fast Wind

*"Most people are starved for the beautiful but don't even
know it. There are some, though, a very few, who do know.
For them, there can never be enough of the beautiful."*
—Art museum docent

Well, it does blow through all events,
maybe, depending on the observer. But across those extents,

it's a blistering and freezing breeze.
It's not the solid stodge of the familiar, pretty as that is,

not the endearing dodge of courtship, not the grope
of youth. It carries, indifferently, one form of hope.

And, hapless lecturer, it will in quantity rush
through your most open and most secret self, there will be push

and crush into whatever slimed,
intermediate steps are called for at the time,

you'll be transferred to re-versions, re-
structures, and not the smallest outcry

or demand will put you elsewhere—not all
that soon, though, possibly. It's a fast wind, the beautiful,

it is Lambda, it is Epsilon,
it has disquieted minds more stalwart than your own

or mine. How far down, really, do you want to know
about that? How often do you want to know?

Genesis

*For Walter H. on the Eliot Elementary School playground
in Tulsa, who jeered at the group of girls playing jacks,
"I'm a boy! God made me all over. You're just a rib!"*

Life, Walt,
is female, from cilia to chitin to the vault

of a skull. As beetle, primate, reptile, smelt:
each species has a single body plan, one gestalt,

the early duplications of which needed only the jolt
of XX. For some lineages, though, caught

in a need to vary themselves against assaults
of predation or climate change (cold, colder, hot)

and for whom it was an onslaught-
advantage to produce more offspring fraught

with changeable traits, males were invented, by alt-
ering the standard plan—probably by not

discarding the occasionally broken molt
of the original autosome. That fault

was pressed into service, the XY a kind of salt
to quicken the XX. Making life for females less difficult

remains to this day your contribution—and thank you. One result
of being breasts deleted down to nipples and the tumult

of genitalia rebuilt
to larger size, is that you intrigue all adult

women: your beauty is half of what they see when they consult
their mirrors. For Life, though, which exalts

itself for itself—I'm sorry if this seems rough—you're more the Alt
key than Control, the version 2 that follows the default.

Cells

*"With enough chips, everything's going to be aware
of us: the door knobs, the stove, probably the chairs
at the coffee shop..."*
—A friend complaining about excesses of the cyber age

The pinched, defiant woman, middle-aged
—at a local ceramics exhibit—enraged

at everyone new or grown, revealed in
the first three minutes of conversation

three things: 1) that she suffers
from fibromyalgia, "treated only with herbs or

teas," her up-chinned expression
slightly pleading but awaiting affirmation

of her frail and necessary superiority;
2) being told I'm interested in cell biology,

that she doesn't "understand cells"
and "can't believe" her body's made of cells;

3) that she disapproves of, unforgivingly,
anyone who fails her needs in any way

—turning dismissively, in my mid-sentence.
Questions about a wooden, dense,

commodiously chip-laden, flat-stare,
human-registering coffeehouse chair

would be these: 1) Can it divert that woman
from her compartmented, lignin-

lined fears? 2) Can it talk to me,
if I like, with a Brobdingnagian vocabulary?

3) Can it teach me something
while being civil and interesting?

If yes, what do I care whether
the dear thing has a wet cell structure?

— V —

Science And The Surround

The Blue Man

A crabapple morning. Two rows
of thin-stemmed trees blow

white balloons; down the street
—beside the car at left and right—

they drop in height and disappear
into a Deco skyscraper

downtown. The air is buffed, like the white-
polish paint on the straight

divider lines. Rectangular light
keeps sliding between the trees like lucite

panes. So, who is he? A blond man,
tall, in overalls, ahead on the right-hand

sidewalk, with a circle of a face.
Blue-capped. Around his blue, barrel waist,

a tool belt. In work boots, he saunters
past flower beds circling like colored water

around the trees. Two lines on his face
cup the sides of his mouth like an embrace.

He could, thoroughly, be
what he appears to be,

Uncle Wonderful, good friend
of Tootle and the Color Kittens,

whose affidavits are not easily
obtained. But the sidewalk breezily

blurs under the leaves a little,
the curb and concrete mottle,

and those might not be smile lines.
They could be the curved, ecliptic plane

on which bitterness is in orbit.
Obsequious, devious, stout,

he could be Snarler,
the bane of wives. Another

toss of blossoms and he's different
—maybe different

with every redoing of the breeze
and light, the flurries

of which can't be entered twice or even
once, for that matter. Which configuration

you stop on
as your estimation of the blue man

will depend on the slant of your
mental shading, bright or dark-striped over

the trees, with its own history
of moment-to-moment mobilities.

Now he's centered in the mirror. Casual
sunshine bounces off a shoulder buckle

and he's Mr. Fuzzy, Rememberer
of Birthdays. Or someone more familiar—

and letting him go is a minute grief
as well as a same-sized instant of relief,

while the sizes of possibilities
rise and fall and he's

maybe always what he seems to be
now: sweetest guy in the world, trust me.

The Ark

*"Why should we invest in a base off the Earth? We should
be solving problems here. We can explore other planets later,
if we have enough resources."*

Marcus Serpentius, at his estate
near Rome, writes to the importunate

Aulus Decius, his long-ago comrade-in-arms,
now in Gaul, managing an extensive farm,

and who's proposed an idea for a machine,
easily portable, for efficient grain

harvesting. "But no one in the Empire
needs such a thing for that work, my dear

Aulus. Even now our captives pour in
from all the conquered lands

and they accomplish everything—stupidly,
with a good deal of waste, admittedly—

but they do it. Why disturb our great economy?
And why now? Not that we couldn't pay

for such a thing: even with depleted silver
from the Iberian mines (*less each year*

of the finest quality, he thinks), there's still
a daily fortune rising into our hands. We'll

have time, Aulus, should a need arise.
We Romans choose our actions when we choose

to choose. You're thinking, I know, of those Huns
and Goths—still massed like incoming stones

from a catapult! But slaves
and silver are what we have

and all we need (*except a thing
or two from the Greeks,* he thought with a pang),

concluding, "Inquire of my good Muguv.
He brings three pheasants and a jug of

my best Falerian." Then to a cooler courtyard,
a table aslant the breeze off his vineyards,

where, shoulders massaged, Marcus
takes up the task of notifying Servius

Gracentius, who'd invested with him to purvey
a Greek wall painting, greatly old, in Thessaly,

that the fragment, said to be intact
—and so valuable!—was in fact

no longer extant. A group portrait, seven feet or wider,
according to the lying trader,

but true that it once stood behind a hilltop peristyle,
the golds and reds visible at half a mile.

Pear Trees

A repeating pattern, this time in
the 1530s, this time a noblewoman in

Capua: accomplished, literate,
accustomed to praise for her unusual wit,

whose consort's connections in the coterie
surrounding Cardinal Schoenberg in Italy

provided her access—limited, of course—
to a sumptuous room in the ecclesiastic palace

on the afternoon when canon Copernicus's
papers—circulating from Poland—would be discussed.

But having placed a gift of sable pears
on a table in that room, as other guests appeared

she stepped behind an arras'd door
to the poplar scent and heated air

undulating up from worn flagstones
crisscrossing under fountains and urns

in the formal garden. The eastern Apennines
stood behind pear trees, one looped with vines,

where a herm of Mercury
flanked her favorite bench. The immobility

of comfort: heat, and the green river slow
along the town's triangular Roman walls below,

the sun-wheel against its blue solid,
the silent, raised terra-cotta beds,

all the repeating hills and reedy plains
down to the steady sea. She did not go in.

Rumors, this and that, had been mentioned
—"heresy," "beauty," "excommunication,"

"the world's and the sun's destruction"—
and there was a calming consolation

in the pear trees repeating exactly
every season; the same birds in the lilac. She

did almost go in, in time—almost.
And, fine-eyed, thirty, for her a later host

of days would allow her to feel, often,
that she was valuable, cherished, genuine.

What she would not feel
—unfortunately?—was the big and real

Earth grow gigantic and then
begin to move beneath her feet and then

to swing around the sun—feel
the body of her mind newly able to fly, central

points floating out to far peripheries,
stars unfixed from their crystal spherity

in space for every thought
to tumble into freely; would not

return later, at will, to that same
air pouring through the collapsing seams

of an erstwhile surrounding box.
Later, a priest, also of the old context,

bored with how long she was taking
and her tears, told her she was forsaking

this mortal coil in a manner suitable and well
done, which provided an instant of comfort. Meanwhile,

at a bench occupied in any garden now
—permeating it and roundabout—

there is, rumor has it, a blooming
wildflower cosmos, its outer meadows caroming,

multidimensioned at every level
(multipetaled, *Compositae*?), shaped by a few initial

conditions, made of minute loops shaking in phase
within a quantized breeze of space,

where the grid of the beautiful is near
but not easily evident, where

joy is indifferent to an indifferent observer,
parsimonious to the parsimonious, where

there is no such thing as a repeating pear,
and, about comfort, where...

   [See note]

66

Mackerel

*To the sunlight coming through the windshield onto
my hands on the steering wheel*

These mackerel-melanin spots
sprayed behind my knuckles, colors caught

in the net of age, their shapes disallowed
for some reason from descriptions of beauty, join the crowd

of events that complain against time
—alien, familiar, multicolored time.

They've come to me, I know, by way of the sun
a few minutes past, in aggregation

with my own past, having sprinkled
the under-spores of a Jurassic cycad, or freckled

the organic sand chipping off a ferric boulder
near a shore of the ever-colder

Tethys Sea. I bequeath them, lightweighted friend, forward
to the mineral-green and sandy world, hard

or soft, now that I'm angled—hesitant—like the cycad,
leaning over new, grainy constructs in the mud.

The Afterlife

In memory of my sister, a nonsmoker who died young of lung cancer, and to a friend who mentioned, after her father's accident, "I hate it, death. Everything's over, you just stop. It's as if you never lived."

I've signed revised documents
creating bequests, spoken with a development

officer for a bench and inscription at a school
in Pennsylvania, heard from a man who'll

build a nesting box, front-lettered "Gayle,"
for bluebirds in his woods near Hale,

Indiana, and I've been made aware,
abruptly, of some family facts, all dark, all austere

but useful—new events that wouldn't be the case,
or expansively connect, if it were still the case

that my desperate, dear sister were alive. An insect,
lovely, its dorsal wings blue-shellacked,

can lower and lift those wings
once or twice on a stem at a turning

of the Orinoco, and within a week
hurricane winds can be about to peak

in the mid-Atlantic. What also happens
—maybe with equal accumulation and extent?—

to those receiving the award
you're funding in your father's name; to hard,

fast breezes across the hemispheres
from blue-winged birds, new every year;

or to young women
reading on a teak bench soon,

at a college, under beech-leaf drop,
when any small wings hesitate, then stop?

On A Rock

Something happened on a low,
rounded rock in a galaxy that tows

and pushes in the Local Group—something
obstreperous, alert, agile, having

the odd, beautiful awkwardness of youth,
made of flyaway matter from deaths

preceding it, now self-sculpting, organized
in open format, feelingly mental, resized,

with a will to swing, hand over hand,
from this near-Orion branch

to treelike limbs in the Perseus
and Cygnus. And the princess,

locked in the cosmos
in the sleep of matter, whose

long and secret name might
include *truth, deep, bright,*

and something else, stirs
in that sleep—just slightly stirs,

afloat in the black lake,
but, if we live, will wake.

Some Generations

"Settlements away from Earth: I'm not sure the human race has the right to propagate itself that far. We might not deserve to go on."

But we are young, just some generations
from the white winds and little, worked stones

of the Pleistocene.
And we have time. At fourteen

billion years, the universe is crisp
and fresh, we've changed down to the grist

and have immensities
of more green time for change. It may be

one of your descendants—deft,
confident, reliable in emotional depth,

able at seventy to learn Chinese
or Navajo in just three weeks,

seriously ill maybe twice
in a two-hundred-year life, spliced

with braking genes to inhibit,
a little, our recidivist

midbrain conflicts and maladaptive
selfishness; better, then, at love

but incomplete still, like all
the sprawling future—who will

discover, say, more dimensions
in non-baryonic matter, their alterations

tumbling and pretty and the result of interaction
with the organic; or some station

of other knowledge that shows
our every summation of life and growth

was based on a scarcity
of variables and too little time. It may be

a child of your child, beautiful,
whose face will grow still

thinking of humanity now, so sweet
and terrible, of our desperate

or patient persistence at efforts
we thought might be pointless, vain, but

continued through every new refrain
of pleasure or loneliness or pain.

Said To Be Possible

If death were a kind of trowel wedging out the stone in the stream—the stone every creature can't help but create by being alive but which inadvertently blocks other lines of flow —there would be little justification for an older adult to object to or fear it.

About that particular fear,
which may be non-"instinctive," there are four

methods I've heard of, as ameliorations.
One: to die like a Roman

after (method two) living like a Greek.
Greek, to move, or try to, even when weak,

toward something excellent, because the human
is what feelingly investigates and learns:

begin piano lessons on a keyboard
laid across the hospital bed.

Roman, about one's life, to assume
it's an intermediate area, an open room,

a changing empire without end or beginning;
to rule, then, without apology, everything

real: consider fear a chimera or belittling inferior
and insist it serve the purpose of your exterior

reputation; decide, if possible, the time of your
death, enact it with bravura

and without an audience. Those are two.
Or: make gifts. Construe

the people around you, their faces,
their turning tones of voice and phrases,

for what they most hope for,
and give it to them. With rearriving fear,

remember those gifts, for a focus. Or,
though it's short, there's method four:

laughter, which doesn't share
its inner cubic spaces with any sort of fear.

These are variants, though—aren't they?—
of the same thing in the same trajectory.

Each is sane, meaning able to let go
of the illusions of starting over or of status quo,

and in each, an energy spirals outward,
away from the self, not inward

and down along the circum-coil
of private dread and panic. In the last of roils

and mess, any of the four might lead
to what's said to be possible: feeling freed

of grievance and greeds, feeling a turn,
pleased to hand the current world's concerns

to the diligence of others. It's my guess
(late in life), that fear of death is a sign of babyness,

of entrenched envies and their sadness
preventing a section of life from seriousness

—too few histones demethylated across the life
as lived, too little maturation other than self-

interest's bindweed. There are sweet decencies,
huge, toward people who are secretly

felt to be extensions of one's self; and there's
the indifference to death that is despair's

gift to unloving parents. But the real thing,
happiness during the last—an organic m-c-squared, pressing

past pain and blur in a condition of ease—
what ways and means for that generosity?

Notes

Lithium, Chromium

In a frigid vacuum, when methanol, ammonia, carbon monoxide and sugar molecules (known to be present in interstellar clouds) are subjected to weeks of bombardment by UV rays and then are brought to room temperature, the water in the mix arranges itself into spheres having the size and structure of cell membranes. This suggests the layered cell-structure of life may form spontaneously in the conditions of space.

A Man, A Boy, A Stick, A Goose With Goslings

Neurotransmitters serotonin and norepinephrine are critical for inscribing our memories of important experiences. In the adult brain, if either chemical is increased at nerve endings in the amygdala and hippocampus, it can trigger a greater flexibility to learn new emotional reactions.

The Carboniferous

The Carboniferous was a section of the Paleozoic when vast coal sediments formed from vegetation. It lasted ca. 120 million years, until the arrival of the Permian world.

The Real

Galaxies, galactic clusters and solar systems are prevented from spinning to pieces by the pushback of dark matter, which is heavy, transparent, incompressible, responsive only to the force of gravity, and composed of something different from ordinary matter.

Horizons

The theory of evolution, already capacious, might also include the slow shaping of human character, which, across a lifetime, shows steady accumulations of emotional cause-and-effect, with adaptive forms and extinctions that can be rapid or slow.

Spherical Eversion

Turning a hollow sphere inside out without making a crease or hole in the sphere has been proven to be possible but remains for now a computer simulation.

Bright Thing Across A Bright Table

In most inflationary-theory accounts of the universe, the near-vacuum of present space was preceded by a colossally energized "false vacuum" of dark energy that destabilized and expanded before the Big Bang. It was during the transition from one vacuum to another that the basic properties of matter were set.

Blue Starred

Our sun, now a middle-aged star at the beginning of its red-giant phase, will double in size across the next billion years. During its expansion, the inner planets may be pushed into temporary orbits around Saturn or Neptune, but eventually all the planets will be vaporized and puffed into interstellar space. Long before then, the outer Kuiper Belt and Oort Cloud may have been colonized by other descendants of the blue-star lineage.

And Snails

A Mother Goose rhyme tells us "frogs and snails and puppy dog tails" are "what little boys are made of," while "sugar and spice and everything nice" are the contents of little girls. Both the old lists are correct as far as they go.

The Good

Enceladus is the outermost of the major Saturnian moons. Volcano Herder is an invention.

The Fast Wind

Lambda is the measurement of dark energy, controlling the expansion rate of the universe. Epsilon is the strength of the force binding protons and neutrons inside an atomic nucleus.

Genesis

"The X and Y sex chromosomes—which arose from a pair of identical, non sex-determining autosomes—diverged from each other over the course of about 300 million years... [The Y chromosome] developed from an X-like ancestor." Bruce Lahn and David Page, "Four Evolutionary Strata on the Human X Chromosome," *Science* 286 (10/29/99): 964-7.

In human embryos, during the sixth week of gestation, if a Y chromosome is present, genes governing the female body plan are activated or suppressed just enough to produce a male.

Cells

When the coffeehouse chair notices that the colors of my outfit are particularly attractive, and tells me it's been giving some thought to what we last talked about and has already sent a provisional order for me to the cashier, then our society may need to reconsider the laws governing marriage.

The Ark

See William E. Burrows, *The Survival Imperative: Using Space to Protect Earth* (New York: Forge/Tom Doherty Associates, 2006).

Pear Trees

...[where], if the equation $m = E/c2$ does not have to be modified, all gardens and benches and women will go on being discrete objects tucked into apparently empty spaces, while, at the quantum level, they will also be fluctuating, twinkling areas of a multidimensional, infinite grid of ever-changing but always coterminous energies, comfortably linked to everything.

Mackerel

The Tethys, a large ocean in the northern hemisphere, was reshaped many times by moving land masses during the Paleozoic and Mesozoic eras. It last closed ca. 225 million years ago but may reopen when the North American plate reaches Asia.

The Afterlife

In complex, changing systems affected by small differences in initial conditions (such as the weather), tiny irregularities can expand into large-scale patterns that are inevitable but not predictable: the "butterfly effect."

On a Rock

See James N. Gardner, *Biocosm* (Maui, Hawaii: Inner Ocean Publishing, Inc., 2003).

Said To Be Possible

See *The Essential Epicurus,* trans. Eugene O'Connor (Buffalo, New York: Prometheus Books, 1993), and Lucretius, *The Nature of Things (De Rerum Natura),* trans. A. E. Stallings (London and New York: Penguin Classics, 2007).

The attachment of damaging methyl molecules to DNA, brought about by environmental stimuli and stress, changes the way a gene is or is not expressed. Methyl groups, however, can sometimes be metabolically altered or detached from DNA after repeated or emphatic experiences that are also epigenetic: a molecular version of hope.

Acknowledgments

Grateful acknowledgment is made to the journals in which these poems appeared, often in earlier versions:

ABZ: "And Snails"
Free Inquiry: "On A Rock"
The Marlboro Review: "Spherical Eversion"
Notre Dame Review: "Blue Starred," "A Man, A Boy, A Stick, A Goose
    With Goslings"
Rhino: "Lithium, Chromium"
Stand Magazine (England): "The Blue Man," "Bright Thing Across
    A Bright Table"

"The Carboniferous" was a finalist for the *The Iowa Review* Poetry Award in 2004.

"Spherical Eversion" was a finalist for *The Marlboro Review* Prize in 2005.

"Some Generations," long-listed in 2005 for the Bridport Prize, was also finalist for the 2008 *Georgetown Review* Magazine Contest.

Science And was a finalist for the 2006 Samuel French Morse Poetry Prize and semifinalist for the 2008 Donald Justice Poetry Prize.

I would like to thank Diane Kistner at FutureCycle Press for her confidence in this project and her fine production work. A special acknowledgment is due to poet and critic Jeredith Merrin, who made most of the visible and invisible conditions for this book possible, including her quoted remarks in "A Man, A Boy, A Stick, A Goose With Goslings." I'm grateful as well, in large equal portions, for two longtime friends, Professor Helen Deutsch at UCLA and Elizabeth Brown Lockman of Green Bank, West Virginia, whose provocative editorial outlooks have been invaluable.

About FutureCycle Press

FutureCycle Press is dedicated to publishing lasting English-language poetry books, chapbooks, and anthologies in both print-on-demand and ebook formats. Founded in 2007 by long-time independent editor/publishers and partners Diane Kistner and Robert S. King, the press incorporated as a nonprofit in 2012. A number of our editors are distinguished poets and writers in their own right, and we have been actively involved in the small press movement going back to the early seventies.

The FutureCycle Poetry Book Prize and honorarium is awarded annually for the best full-length volume of poetry we publish in a calendar year. Introduced in 2013, our Good Works projects are anthologies devoted to issues of universal significance, with all proceeds donated to a related worthy cause. Our Selected Poems series highlights contemporary poets with a substantial body of work to their credit; with this series we strive to resurrect work that has had limited distribution or is now out of print.

We are dedicated to giving all of the authors we publish the care their work deserves, making our catalog of titles the most diverse and distinguished it can be, and paying forward any earnings to fund more great books.

We've learned a few things about independent publishing over the years. We've also evolved a unique, resilient publishing model that allows us to focus mainly on vetting and preserving for posterity the most books of exceptional quality without becoming overwhelmed with bookkeeping and mailing, fundraising activities, or taxing editorial and production "bubbles." To find out more about what we are doing, come see us at www.futurecycle.org.

The FutureCycle Poetry Book Prize

All full-length volumes of poetry published by FutureCycle Press in a given calendar year are considered for the annual FutureCycle Poetry Book Prize. This allows us to consider each submission on its own merits, outside of the context of a contest. Too, the judges see the finished book, which will have benefitted from the beautiful book design and strong editorial gloss we are famous for.

The book ranked the best in judging is announced as the prize-winner in the subsequent year. There is no fixed monetary award; instead, the winning poet receives an honorarium of 20% of the total net royalties from all poetry books and chapbooks the press sold online in the year the winning book was published. The winner is also accorded the honor of being on the panel of judges for the next year's competition and, in this capacity, receives a copy of all books in contention for that year's prize.

www.ingramcontent.com/pod-product-compliance
Lightning Source LLC
Chambersburg PA
CBHW070008100426
42741CB00012B/3160